CW01083047

THE STRAY SHOPPING CARTS OF EASTERN NORTH AMERICA: A GUIDE TO FIELD IDENTIFICATION

ACKNOWLEDGMENTS
I would like to thank the various organizations and institutions that have given me opportunities
develop and show this project: Hallwalls Contemporary Arts Center, Buffalo, New York; Big Orb
Soundlab, Buffalo, New York; the International Studio & Curatorial Program, New York, New Yor
Real Art Ways, Hartford, Connecticut; and Spaces Gallery, Cleveland, Ohio. Special thanks to Black
White Gallery, Brooklyn, New York, and to everyone at Abrams. Many thanks go to my wife, Colet
my family, and Toby Montague for all his unpaid labor.

THE
STRAY
SHOPPING
CARTS OF EASTERN
NORTH AMERICA
A GUIDE TO FIELD IDENTIFICATION

JULIAN MONTAGUE

ABRAMS IMAGE

Editor: Deborah Aaronson
Designer: Julian Montague
Production Manager: Maria Pia Gramaglia

Library of Congress Cataloging-in-Publication Data

Montague, Julian.
   The stray shopping carts of Eastern North America : a guide to field
   identification / Julian Montague.
      p. cm.
   ISBN 0-8109-5520-2 (flexibind)
   1. Photography, Artistic. 2. Shopping carts—North America—Pictorial
works. 3. Montague, Julian.   I. Title.
TR655.M66 2006
779.092—dc22
                                        2005024154

Printed and bound in China

10 9 8 7 6 5 4 3 2 1

harry n. abrams, inc.
115 West 18th Street
New York, NY 10011
www.hnabooks.com

Harry N. Abrams, Inc. is a subsidiary of

↘ TABLE OF CONTENTS

INTRODUCTION

THE STRAY SHOPPING CART IDENTIFICATION SYSTEM

Over the last several decades, the stray shopping cart has quietly become an integral part of the urban and suburban landscapes of the industrialized world. To the average person, the stray shopping cart is most often thought of as a signifier of urban blight or as an indicator of a consumer society gone too far. Unfortunately, the acceptance of these oversimplified designations has discouraged any serious examination of the stray shopping cart phenomenon.

Until now, the major obstacle that has prevented people from thinking critically about stray shopping carts has been that we have not had any formalized language to differentiate one shopping cart from another.

In order to encourage a more nuanced and comprehensive understanding of the phenomenon, I have worked for the past six years to develop a system of identification for stray shopping carts. Unlike a Linaean taxonomy, which is based on the shared physical characteristics of living things, this system works by defining the various states and situations in which stray shopping carts can be found. The categories of classification were arrived at by observing shopping carts in different situations and considering the conditions and human motives that have placed carts in specific situations and the potential for a cart to transition from one situation to another.

The resulting Stray Shopping Cart Identification System consists of two classes and thirty-three subtypes that can be used singly or in combination to describe and thereby "identify" any found cart. One of the unfortunate difficulties in implementing a situational taxonomy of this kind is that one is often required to speculate about where a cart is coming from and where it is going next. While this uncertainty can at times be vexing, it must be remembered that this system is the first attempt to categorize and analyze the transient nature of the shopping cart. The refinement of this system is an ongoing process.

This book is a starting point for those interested in understanding and becoming sensitive to a dynamic part of their environment. Whether used in the field or simply read at home, this book will quickly give the amateur cart observer the tools needed to identify the stray shopping carts in his or her area.

ABOUT THIS BOOK

This guide is divided into five sections with one appendix. SECTION 1: INTRODUCTION (pp. 6–13) explains the basic concepts and terminology of the Stray Shopping Cart Identification System. Also included is a subsection that addresses the use of the System beyond Eastern North America. An annotated Transitional Sequence Diagram can be found on pages 12–13.

SECTION 2: CLASS A: FALSE STRAYS / TYPES 1–11 (pp. 14–27) and SECTION 3: CLASS B: TRUE STRAYS / TYPES 1–22 (pp. 28–51) define and illustrate the TYPES that make up the System of Identification.

SECTION 4: SELECTED SPECIMENS (pp. 52–165) serves three purposes: 1) to demonstrate the diversity of stray shopping cart activity; 2) to show, via the TYPE icons and explanatory text, how the System should be used; and 3) to sensitize the eye to the various ways that stray shopping carts appear in the environment. The section presents 197 documented specimens in no particular order. 84 images have explanatory text while the other 112 have only their type designations. The photographs of the carts can not always communicate all of the contextual information that has led to the assigning of specific type designations, however, they are useful for purposes 1 and 2.

SECTION 5: THE NIAGARA RIVER GORGE: ANALYZING A COMPLEX VANDALISM SUPER SITE (pp. 166–175) shows how the System can be used to investigate site-specific stray shopping cart activity.

APPENDIX A: RELATED PHENOMENA (p. 176) provides a brief profile of three objects (stray plastic bags, discarded tires, stray traffic cones) that are often found near stray shopping carts and share some of their transitional patterns.

NOTE: None of the photographs in this book were staged; all shopping carts were documented in situ.

IMAGE REFERENCE KEY

When a specific image from a multi-image page in either SECTION 4 or 5 is referenced elsewhere in the book, it is referred to by the page number and an A, B, or C (see left). For example: see p.123/C.

↘ CONCEPTS / TERMINOLOGY

SOURCE	
Any business that uses shopping carts in a conventional manner.	CLOSED SOURCE: A SOURCE that has gone out of business.
	SOURCE AGENTS: Employees or subcontractors of the SOURCE who collect and return stray carts.

CLASS A: FALSE STRAYS

1) A shopping cart that while on the SOURCE lot is diverted from its primary function, damaged, or otherwise rendered useless.

2) A shopping cart that appears to be a stray cart but that is ultimately returned to service in the SOURCE from which it originated.

CLASS B: TRUE STRAYS

1) A cart that will not be returned to the SOURCE from which it originated.

2) CLASS B: TRUE STRAY TYPES may be used as secondary designations for CLASS A: FALSE STRAY specimens.

TYPES	SPECIMEN
The subdivisions of CLASSES A and B. (There are currently 11 CLASS A TYPES and 22 CLASS B TYPES included in the System.)	A cart that has been photographically documented and assigned a single or multiple TYPE designations.

ICONS

A/2 B/2	B/12	SU	R→
The subdivisions of CLASSES A and B, abbreviated by using the CLASS letter alone with the TYPE number.	A green CLASS B TYPE icon with a brown border represents a secondary CLASS B TYPE designation.	SOURCE UNKNOWN	DESIGNATION RETAINED

When an image contains multiple carts and there is no notation indicating otherwise, the TYPE designations should be assumed to refer to all carts in the image.

GAP SPACES	Vacant lots, ditches, spaces between buildings, behind buildings, under bridges and overpasses, and all manner of vacant GAPS between properties, public or private.

⬊ NOTES ON IDENTIFICATION

Because the Stray Shopping Cart Identification System considers the situation a stray cart is in and the potential to transition to new situations, it is often not possible to assign TYPE designations with complete certainty. Some TYPES, B/2 DAMAGED for example, describe the physical condition the stray cart is in; consequently it is relatively easy to assign the B/2 TYPE designation. TYPES that describe a cart's situation in a larger context (A/9 REMOTE FALSE, B/1 OPEN TRUE, and many others) cannot be assigned with certainty without actively tracking the cart for days or weeks. With long-term tracking often being out of the question, the observer should take into account the context in which he/she finds the cart and construct a likely hypothesis.

One must keep in mind that a number of TYPES have significant overlap in their definitions. For example, a B/3 FRAGMENT is by definition also a B/2 DAMAGED. Similarly, B/10 PLOW CRUSH and B/11 TRAIN DAMAGED are also B/2 DAMAGED. The overlap is useful in situations where the specific cause of the damage cannot be determined. In such cases, the B/2 TYPE alone should be assigned. At some level, it would be correct to think of B/3, B/10, B/11, and B/20 as subtypes of B/2. However, given that this System is based on the situation in which a cart is found, these TYPES must be separate. When assigning TYPE designations, it is not necessary to assign redundant TYPES. For example, one does not need to assign B/2 DAMAGED as well as B/10 PLOW CRUSH.

Another aspect of the identification process is that a cart may hold multiple TYPE designations. For example, a B/14 ARCHAIC cart can simultaneously be a B/10 PLOW CRUSH. Some TYPE designations, once acquired by a specimen, are retained (indicated by the R–ARROW icon) throughout all subsequent transitions, while others are lost when a transition occurs. For example, if a B/3 FRAGMENT is thrown in the trash, it will acquire the B/19 IN/AS REFUSE designation, but it will still retain the B/3 designation. When a B/4 ON/AS PERSONAL PROPERTY is removed from personal property, the designation is not retained. A general rule is that physically damaged or modified carts retain the TYPES that affected them, while those TYPES based purely on the situational context in which they are found are lost when a transition to a new situation occurs. One TYPE outside of this dichotomy is B/14 ARCHAIC, which is always retained since it is defined by the irreversible event of its SOURCE of origin closing.

CLASS A TYPES can be subject to some CLASS B TYPES. A common example is that when an A/1 CLOSE FALSE is vandalized at the edge of the SOURCE lot, it acquires the secondary TYPE of B/12 SIMPLE VANDALISM. Such situations are indicated by a green icon with a brown border. A CLASS B cart can acquire a CLASS A TYPE only when a B/1 OPEN TRUE is left at a bus stop, where it becomes A/3 BUS STOP DISCARD.

⬊ GEOGRAPHIC RELEVANCE

The primary research for the development of the Stray Shopping Cart Identification System was done in Buffalo, New York, over the course of six years. The Buffalo area was used as a systemic template due to its high level of cart activity and the drastic seasonal changes that allow the presence of snow-related TYPES. Further research and experimental applications of the System have been done at various locations in the Eastern United States and Southern Canada. While the System appears to work in most locations in the East, there is the possibility that some regions may possess conditions and forces not considered in the present version. The System is not closed and new discoveries that do not fall under the currently defined TYPES will demand the establishment of new TYPES.

WESTERN NORTH AMERICA—Although the System has not been tested or widely applied in the Western United States, Canada, or Mexico, it is probable that the System in its present form would encompass the majority of Western stray cart activity. Recent research done on the Hawaiian islands of Oahu and Maui prove that the System is fully applicable at the most remote western reaches of the United States (see below).

EUROPE—Recent travels have confirmed that the System of Identification functions beyond the North American continent. FALSE and TRUE strays were found in three Scandinavian capitals: Copenhagen, Oslo, and Stockholm, and on the Swedish island of Gotland. While the stray activity in these cities differs in intensity from that of an Eastern North American city, the basic TYPE designations of the System appear to accurately describe it. There was, however, one important exception found in Copenhagen (see right). Anecdotal reports from elsewhere in Europe suggest that the System may function continentwide.

ASIA, AUSTRALIA, SOUTH AMERICA—The System has not yet been tested on these continents.

⬊ THE HAWAIIAN ISLANDS

The System has recently been tested on the Hawaiian islands of Oahu and Maui. Both islands featured a fairly high level of stray shopping cart activity. The range of TYPES found were similar to what one would find in the Southeastern United States.

The specimen at right is an A/3 BUS STOP DISCARD found on the windward side of Oahu. See p. 102/A for an additional Hawaiian specimen.

↘ AN ENDEMIC TYPE / COIN RETURN IN COPENHAGEN

In Copenhagen, Denmark, the coin return key on some locking carts is the same size as the key for the coin return mechanism on the city's public bicycles. This means that a person can appropriate a cart from a SOURCE and then, some distance away, get their coin returned by locking the cart to a bicycle rack. It also means that a cart can be appropriated, with a coin, from a bicycle rack. The present System does not have a TYPE or combination of TYPES that describe this phenomenon.

↘ 3 HYPOTHETICAL TRANSITIONAL SEQUENCES (ANNOTATED)

This Transitional Sequence Diagram is a graphic depiction of the way in which a stray shopping cart acquires and loses TYPE designations.

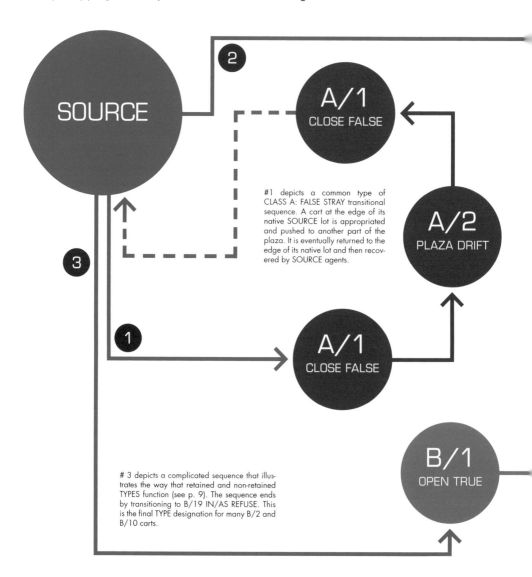

SOURCE

2

A/1
CLOSE FALSE

A/2
PLAZA DRIFT

#1 depicts a common type of CLASS A: FALSE STRAY transitional sequence. A cart at the edge of its native SOURCE lot is appropriated and pushed to another part of the plaza. It is eventually returned to the edge of its native lot and then recovered by SOURCE agents.

3

1

A/1
CLOSE FALSE

B/1
OPEN TRUE

3 depicts a complicated sequence that illustrates the way that retained and non-retained TYPES function (see p. 9). The sequence ends by transitioning to B/19 IN/AS REFUSE. This is the final TYPE designation for many B/2 and B/10 carts.

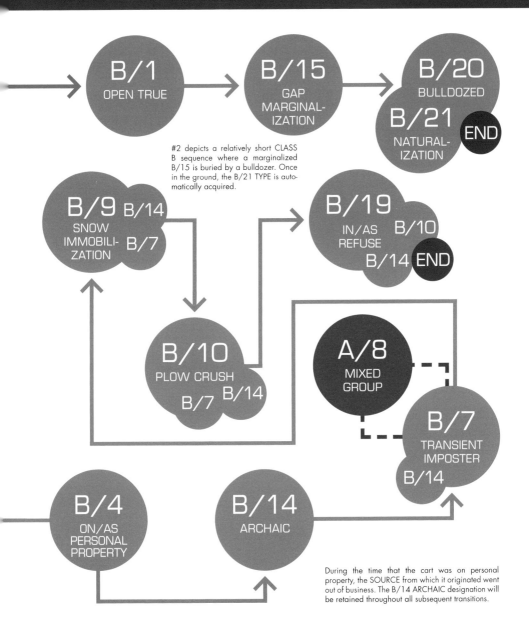

B/1
OPEN TRUE

B/15
GAP MARGINAL-IZATION

B/20
BULLDOZED

B/21
NATURAL-IZATION

END

#2 depicts a relatively short CLASS B sequence where a marginalized B/15 is buried by a bulldozer. Once in the ground, the B/21 TYPE is automatically acquired.

B/9 **B/14**
SNOW IMMOBILI-ZATION **B/7**

B/19
IN/AS REFUSE **B/10**
B/14 END

B/10
PLOW CRUSH
B/7 **B/14**

A/8
MIXED GROUP

B/7
TRANSIENT IMPOSTER
B/14

B/4
ON/AS PERSONAL PROPERTY

B/14
ARCHAIC

During the time that the cart was on personal property, the SOURCE from which it originated went out of business. The B/14 ARCHAIC designation will be retained throughout all subsequent transitions.

CLASS A ↓ →

TYPES 1–11

FALSE STRAYS

1) A shopping cart that while on the SOURCE lot is diverted from its primary function, damaged, or otherwise rendered useless.

2) A shopping cart that appears to be a stray cart but that is ultimately returned to service in the SOURCE from which it originated.

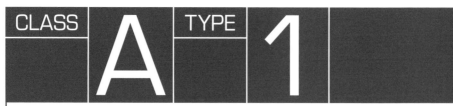

CLASS	A	TYPE	1

CLOSE FALSE

→ A cart found at the edge of the SOURCE parking lot or within a two-block radius.

→ Often found in ditches, on median strips, and on grassy areas adjacent to the SOURCE parking lot.

→ A/1 carts are often subject to acts of B/12 SIMPLE VANDALISM.

↑ A/1 This specimen was found just beyond the edge of its native SOURCE lot.

CLASS A TYPE 2

PLAZA DRIFT

→ A cart situated in a foreign lot connected to the SOURCE lot by the continuous pavement of a shopping plaza.

→ Will be collected by SOURCE agents.

→ NOTE: An A/2 cart is often subject to A/4 DAMAGED AT SOURCE and A/6 PLOW CRUSH AT SOURCE designations.

A/2

A typical example of an A/2, this specimen was found in front of a foreign plaza-connected SOURCE.

CLASS	**A**	TYPE	**3**

BUS STOP DISCARD

→ A cart or group of carts found close to a bus stop, subway entrance, trolley stop, or train station that is within a block of the SOURCE lot.

→ B/3 carts are often turned on their sides and used as benches.

→ A/3 may be used as a secondary TYPE designation when a B/1 OPEN TRUE cart is found at a public transportation stop. This is the only instance where a CLASS A TYPE may be used as a secondary designation for a CLASS B TYPE. This is indicated by an A/3 icon with a green border.

A/3 These A/3 specimens have been turned on their sides and used as benches. Note how the sides have been made concave by the sitters.

CLASS A TYPE 4

(R→)

DAMAGED AT SOURCE

→ A damaged cart situated within the SOURCE parking lot.

→ Structural integrity often compromised beyond repair.

→ Damaged by collisions with cars, trucks, or snowplows.

→ Will likely be sent to the scrap yard or dump.

→ Separate fragments resulting from damage become A/7 FRAGMENTS.

↑ A/2 A/4 Note that the damage to the specimen has resulted in the creation of numerous fragments. These are each considered to be separate A/7 FRAGMENTS.

A
5

DAMAGED GROUP

→ Damaged carts grouped behind or beside the SOURCE building by SOURCE agents.

→ Will likely be stripped for parts and/or sent to the scrap yard or dump.

→ Transitions to A/8 MIXED GROUP with the addition of two or more foreign carts.

↑ A/5 In northern regions, one is more likely to find A/5 groups in the early spring when the cumulative effects of the harsh conditions of winter can be observed.

CLASS A TYPE 6

R→

PLOW CRUSH AT SOURCE

→ A cart destroyed in SOURCE lot by snowplows.

→ Structural integrity compromised beyond repair.

→ Will likely be stripped for parts and/or sent to the scrap yard or dump.

→ Rarely occurs in the southern regions of the United States.

↑ A/6   This specimen was found at the top of a 12-foot snow pile.

CLASS A TYPE 7

R→

FRAGMENTS AT SOURCE

→ An A/4 DAMAGED AT SOURCE or an A/6 PLOW CRUSH AT SOURCE cart consisting of 50% or less of its original structure.

→ Most commonly associated with A/6 PLOW CRUSH.

→ NOTE: In the event that multiple pieces are broken off of an A/4 or A/6 equaling less than 50% of the original structure, the separated pieces become A/7 FRAGMENTS AT SOURCE, while the remaining structure retains the A/4 or A/6 designation.

↑ A/7 As these A/7 PLOW CRUSH FRAGMENTS demonstrate, plastic carts are subject to more severe fragmentation than metal carts.

CLASS **A** TYPE **8**

MIXED GROUP

→ A mix of FALSE and TRUE carts often situated behind a SOURCE building.

→ Carts are gathered and situated by SOURCE agents in an effort to remove damaged and non-native carts from a parking lot or plaza.

→ Additions are often made to A/8 MIXED GROUPS by citizens who collect stray carts from their neighborhoods and leave them at the nearest SOURCE.

↑ A/8 | This A/8 was found behind a shopping mall.

CLASS A TYPE 9

REMOTE FALSE

→ A cart situated on a sidewalk or street outside of a two-block radius of the SOURCE.

→ Will likely be recovered by the SOURCE'S collection trucks.

→ Impossible to differentiate from B/1 OPEN TRUE without long-term observation and tracking.

↑ A/9 This A/9 was found .25 miles from its SOURCE.

CLASS A TYPE 10

ALTERNATIVE USAGE

→ Native carts used by a SOURCE in an unconventional manner.

→ Includes carts used as parking-lot markers, temporary fencing, door stops, tool boxes, etc.

A/10 These A/10 specimens appear to have been tied to the fence in order to keep the snowplow operator from burying the drainage gutter in snow.

CLASS A TYPE 11

FALSE GROUP

→ Groups of FALSE STRAYS found near and around apartment buildings and housing complexes close to the SOURCE.

→ Will likely be recovered by SOURCE agents.

→ Groups are often formed by building staff in the expectation that they will be recovered by SOURCE agents.

A/11 | This A/11 GROUP was found behind a large apartment building.

TRUE STRAYS

1) A cart that will not be returned to the SOURCE from which it originated.

2) CLASS B: TRUE STRAY TYPES may be used as secondary designations for CLASS A: FALSE STRAY specimens.

OPEN TRUE

→ A cart situated on a street or sidewalk, or in a park or parking lot, outside of a two-block SOURCE radius.

→ Impossible to differentiate from A/9 REMOTE FALSE.

→ All TRUE STRAY carts theoretically transition through and retain the B/1 designation, thus all CLASS B TYPES are B/1 OPEN TRUE.

↑ B/1 This specimen was found four miles from its SOURCE of origin.

CLASS B / TYPE 2

R→

DAMAGED

→ A cart damaged by violent encounters with cars, trucks, snowplows, trains, earth-moving equipment, etc., or by acts of B/12 SIMPLE and B/13 COMPLEX VANDALISM.

→ Structural integrity often compromised beyond repair.

→ Situated at least one block from the SOURCE.

→ TYPES B/3, B/10, B/11, and B/20 are by definition also B/2.

B/1 B/2
This specimen was most likely damaged in an encounter with a car or truck.

FRAGMENT

→ A cart damaged by violent encounters with cars, trucks, snowplows, trains, earth-moving equipment, etc., or by acts of B/12 SIMPLE and B/13 COMPLEX VANDALISM.

→ Consists of 50% or less of its original structure.

→ NOTE: When multiple pieces are broken off of a B/2 DAMAGED equaling less than 50% of the original structure, the separated pieces become B/3s, while the remaining structure retains the B/2 designation.

B/3 B/11 SU

This specimen was found near a set of railroad tracks. An investigation of the immediate area did not yield any related fragments.

CLASS B TYPE 4

R→

ON/AS PERSONAL PROPERTY

→ A cart appropriated by private individuals for personal use.

→ Found on personal property: garages, yards, apartment building courtyards, etc.

→ This TYPE includes appropriation by the homeless.

→ It can be difficult to differentiate between B/4 and B/5 ON/AS BUSINESS PROPERTY carts in the case of carts in and around apartment buildings.

↑ (B/4) (B/14) This specimen was found in a suburban garage. The appropriation of STRAY carts for home use appears to be a widespread practice.

CLASS	B	TYPE	5

ON/AS BUSINESS PROPERTY

→ A cart appropriated by a commercial enterprise for an unconventional use. This does not include the supplying of carts to customers for their use. See B/6 ASSIMILATED.

↑ (B/5) This specimen was found in a thrift store being used to display used records. The same store also has a large number of B/6 ASSIMILATED carts from several different SOURCES. Because this specimen is being used in an unconventional manner, it can be considered a B/5 ON/AS BUSINESS PROPERTY.

CLASS B TYPE 6

ASSIMILATED

→ Any TRUE STRAY appropriated knowingly or accidentally by a SOURCE business for conventional shopping cart use.

→ Easily misidentified when a SOURCE legitimately purchases the carts of another SOURCE.

→ ASSIMILATED carts are subject to CLASS A TYPE designations.

B/6 B/14 The red cart is the B/6; it is also B/14 ARCHAIC.

TRANSIENT IMPOSTER

→ A B/1 OPEN TRUE found on a foreign SOURCE lot.

→ Often the result of people attempting to clear sidewalks and streets of B/1 OPEN TRUE carts.

→ NOTE: B/7 carts often transition to B/15 GAP MARGINALIZATION and B/15 EDGE MARGINALIZATION.

↑ B/7 B/14 The cart on the left is a B/7. It is also an unusually old B/14 ARCHAIC from a SOURCE that closed 15 years prior to documentation.

STRUCTURALLY MODIFIED

→ A cart physically modified to allow alternative utilitarian functions.

→ Often involves the removal of the lower chassis of a stray cart that is then used as a base for a custom-built cart.

→ Both the used and discarded cart pieces are assigned the B/8 designation.

→ B/8 often produces B/3 FRAGMENTS.

↑ B/8 B/14 The rear wheels on this specimen have been replaced with what appear to be lawn mower wheels and the bottom rear third of the basket has been cut away; to what purpose is unknown.

CLASS B TYPE 9
SNOW IMMOBILIZATION

→ An A/9 REMOTE FALSE or B/1 OPEN TRUE cart immobilized by heavy snowfall.

→ Immobility facilitates transition to various CLASS B TYPES, most notably B/10 PLOW CRUSH.

→ Often used as a secondary designation for CLASS A carts.

→ Rarely occurs in the southern regions of the United States.

 B/1 B/9 This specimen was documented in Buffalo, New York, after a snowfall of three feet. Sudden heavy snows have what might be termed a "Pompeii Effect," wherein all stray shopping cart movement is frozen. Such times offer an opportunity to assess stray shopping cart activity patterns.

CLASS B TYPE 10

R→

PLOW CRUSH

→ A TRUE STRAY destroyed by snowplows.

→ Structural integrity compromised beyond repair.

→ B/7 TRANSIENT IMPOSTERS often transition to B/10.

→ Rarely occurs in the southern regions of the United States.

↑ B/7 B/10 This specimen B/7 TRANSIENT IMPOSTER was found on top of an eight-foot plow-created snow pile.

TRAIN DAMAGED

→ A cart destroyed by encounters with trains, always fragmented by force of impact.

→ Often situated on train tracks by vandals. See B/12 SIMPLE VANDALISM and B/13 COMPLEX VANDALISM.

→ Usually differentiated from other TYPES of damaged carts (A/4, A/6, A/7, B/2, B/3, B/10) by the proximity to train tracks and the extreme nature of the physical damage.

↑ B/3 B/11 SU

The pretzel-like shape of this B/3 FRAGMENT, B/11 TRAIN DAMAGED specimen illustrates the severity of a cart-train encounter.

SIMPLE VANDALISM

→ A cart purposefully damaged and/or radically resituated by vandals.

→ An act requiring no more than two steps to complete—an impulsive act.

→ Often involves pushing/throwing carts into bodies of water, down hills or embankments, down stairs, or off bridges.

↑ B/12 This specimen is a relatively rare example of a B/12 that involves moving a cart upward. In the majority of cases, carts are resituated in a downward direction.

CLASS B TYPE 13

COMPLEX VANDALISM

→ A cart purposefully damaged and/or radically resituated by vandals.

→ Differentiated from B/12 SIMPLE VANDALISM by the degree of complexity and effort required to resituate the cart.

→ EXAMPLES: Pushing a cart to the river and then pushing it in is B/12 SIMPLE VANDALISM. Pushing a cart to the river, lifting a cart over a six-foot fence, and then pushing it into the river is B/13 COMPLEX VANDALISM.

B/13 B/17 These B/13 COMPLEX VANDALISM specimens were found in a public swimming pool. The three steps that make their situation B/13 are: 1) the initial appropriation, 2) lifting the carts over a seven-foot fence, and 3) pushing the carts into the pool.

CLASS B TYPE 14

R→

ARCHAIC

→ Any cart from a SOURCE that is no longer in business.

→ NOTE: Because the transition to a B/14 designation is contingent only on the closing of the SOURCE, any CLASS B cart can become a B/14 in addition to any other TYPE designations.

↑ B/14 B/15 The SOURCE from which this specimen originated closed four years prior to documentation.

CLASS B TYPE 15
GAP MARGINALIZATION

→ A cart situated in a vacant lot or ditch, between buildings, behind a building, in a doorway, under a bridge or overpass, or in any manner of vacant public GAP between properties.

→ Moved into GAP spaces in an effort to marginalize carts that have become nuisances.

→ Carts can be placed in GAP situations and spaces when rough terrain forces a person to abort an attempt to cross a vacant space with a cart.

B/15 B/18 The combination of B/15 GAP MARGINALIZATION and B/18 AS REFUSE RECEPTACLE is not uncommon.

CLASS B TYPE 16
EDGE MARGINALIZATION

→ A cart removed from personal or private property to just beyond the property line.

→ Often moved to the opposite side of a fence in an effort to marginalize carts that have become nuisances.

This specimen was marginalized from a shopping plaza parking lot.

B/16   SU

CLASS B TYPE 17

REMOTE GROUP

→ Three or more CLASS B carts grouped in vacant lots, post-industrial areas, and illegal dump sites.

→ Often found in GAP spaces.

B/17 This B/17 REMOTE GROUP was found behind a closed SOURCE.

AS REFUSE RECEPTACLE

→ A cart used as a refuse receptacle by individuals, businesses, or the public collectively.

→ B/18 differs from B/19 IN/AS REFUSE by containing at least twice the refuse that appears on the ground around it.

→ B/18 and B/19 TYPE designations can occur simultaneously.

B/7 **B/18** **SU** — This B/7 TRANSIENT IMPOSTER was found behind a SOURCE building on a foreign SOURCE lot.

CLASS B TYPE 19

IN/AS REFUSE

→ Situated in and around trash cans, dumpsters, scrap heaps, or illegal dump sites.

→ The majority of CLASS B carts will ultimately transition to B/19.

B/19 SU | B/19 is often the final TYPE in a cart's transitional sequence.

CLASS **B** TYPE **20**

R→

BULLDOZED

→ A cart buried, crushed, or otherwise resituated by earth-moving equipment.

→ Occurs during development of GAP spaces, post-industrial areas, and illegal dump sites.

→ Once in its resting place, a B/20 automatically acquires the B/21 NATURALIZATION designation.

B/3 B/12 B/20 B/21 SU

This B/3 FRAGMENT, B/20 BULLDOZED, B/21 NATURALIZATION specimen was found on the site of a bridge reconstruction project. The cart was situated beneath the original bridge through an act of B/12 SIMPLE VANDALISM.

CLASS B TYPE 21

NATURALIZATION

→ A cart resituated by natural forces.

→ Most commonly, carts that have been situated in bodies of water by B/12 SIMPLE or B/13 COMPLEX VANDALISM and are subsequently moved by river currents, buried in silt, or crushed by ice.

→ This TYPE includes carts resituated by tornadoes, hurricanes, floods, earthquakes, landslides, and other natural disasters.

B/13 B/21 SU This specimen has been buried by silt and is encrusted with zebra mussels. It was found in a canal adjacent to Lake Erie. An evaluation of the access points to the canal strongly suggest that the cart was placed in the water by an act of B/13 COMPLEX VANDALISM.

WHEEL LOCK STRAY

→ A cart with a wheel lock mechanism found outside of a two-block SOURCE radius.

→ NOTE: The practice of fitting carts with locking mechanisms is currently on the rise; it is not yet understood how this will effect stray activity in the future.

↑ B/7 B/14 B/22 | Despite its locked wheel, this specimen traveled at least 1.5 miles from where its native SOURCE once was. The SOURCE closed six months prior to documentation.

SELECTED ⤋ →

This section features stray shopping carts photographically
documented and identified using the System.

SPECIMENS

 B/12 SU

This specimen was thrown into a drainage ditch in an act of B/12 SIMPLE VANDALISM.

 B/14 B/16 SU

 B/1 B/2

   B/4 B/17

This B/4 ON/AS PERSONAL PROPERTY, B/17 REMOTE GROUP was found inside the courtyard of an apartment building for the elderly in Charleston, South Carolina. The carts are corralled for repeated use.

  B/5

   B/2 B/14

These specimens were found in a disused loading dock that had flooded with rainwater and melted snow.

This B/12 SIMPLE VANDALISM, B/21 NATURALIZATION specimen has been resituated by the movement of the river. The amount of attached organic material suggests that it has been in the river for some time.

The melting of plow-created snow piles can reveal multiple levels of CLASS A and CLASS B PLOW CRUSHES. This A/8 MIXED GROUP contains A/6 PLOW CRUSH AT SOURCE, A/7 FRAGMENTS AT SOURCE, and B/10 PLOW CRUSHES. In this case, the B/10 icon refers to the CLASS B specimens in the A/8, and therefore does not require a brown border.

A/9

This specimen was found next to a bicycle path. It is situated at the top of a steep riverbank, which suggests an increased potential for transition to CLASS B via an act of B/12 SIMPLE VANDALISM.

  B/5

  A/9

This B/5 ON/AS BUSINESS PROPERTY specimen was found on the site of a closed SOURCE that was in the process of being prepared for reopening under new management. The cart is being used to hold up a temporary fence. This situation is similar to A/10 ALTERNATIVE USAGE.

  B/2 B/13 SU

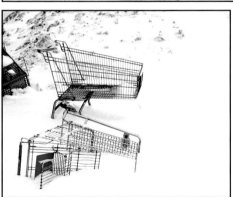

This B/19 IN/AS REFUSE specimen was found on an industrial site that had fallen into partial disuse. It is unclear whether or not the cart had been in use on the site or if it was a nuisance cart that had been marginalized.

↖ B/3 B/7 B/8 B/15

It is not uncommon to find carts that have had their lower structures sawed off (see inset). The lower structure is usually used to construct a new, specialized cart (see pp.140–141, p.159/A). This particular specimen was found in a GAP space next to a SOURCE lot to which it was not native. This situation makes it a B/15 GAP MARGINALIZED cart as well as a B/3 FRAGMENT, B/7 TRANSIENT IMPOSTER, and a B/8 STRUCTURALLY MODIFIED.

  B/10

Although there was no snow present at the time of documentation, the large tire tracks (consistent with a front loader) and extreme damage done to the cart's structure, suggest that the specimen is a B/10 PLOW CRUSH.

 B/9

 A/2 A/7

  B/13

This specimen was found in a river near its native SOURCE lot. It has been assigned the B/13 COMPLEX VANDALISM because in order to reach the water with the cart, the vandals had to push it through a long stretch of grass. Note that the traffic marker was vandalized in a similar way.

   B/6 B/17

   A/9 B/15

This specimen is an example of how a cart can be placed in a B/15 GAP MARGINALIZATION situation by a person or persons abandoning a cart when the terrain becomes too rough or they are blocked by a fence or similar obstacle (see p. 87/A).

This specimen is a typical metal B/11 TRAIN DAMAGED. It is a B/3 FRAGMENT—the force of impact has eliminated most of the straight lines from the original structure. It was most likely situated on the tracks via an act of B/12 SIMPLE VANDALISM.

  B/5

This B/5 ON/AS BUSINESS PROPERTY specimen was found being used to store a coiled hose on the grounds of a large apartment building.

  B/12

  B/3 SU

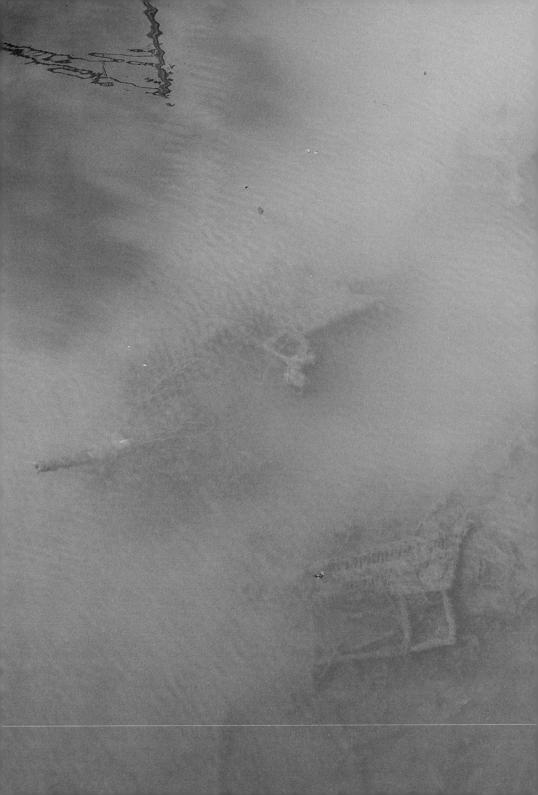

Through multiple acts of B/12 SIMPLE VANDALISM, this B/17 REMOTE GROUP was formed below an urban bridge. Over time the river's currents moved the carts downstream, which enabled the B/21 NATURALIZED designation. The naturalization process provides a clue that tells us that these carts were not all thrown into the river at the same time; the carts at the top of the frame are farther away from the bridge than a person or persons could physically throw a cart. Note the vandalized street sign on the far right.

   B/3 SU

This B/3 FRAGMENT was found partially buried in a stream-bed. A thorough knowledge of the structural design of the various models of shopping carts is essential to spotting B/3 FRAGMENTS.

  B/5

   B/1 B/7

   (A/1) (B/12)

The lower cart is an A/1 CLOSE FALSE. The placement of the native cart into the A/1 is a mild act of B/12 SIMPLE VANDALISM.

   (B/14) (B/16)

    (B/6) (B/10) (SU)

↖ B/12

This B/12 SIMPLE VANDALISM specimen was pushed down an embankment from a bicycle path.

Due to the fact that the SOURCE for this specimen is unknown, one cannot be certain if it is a TRUE or FALSE stray. The conditions in the plaza where is was found suggest that it is an A/2 PLAZA DRIFT, A/4 DAMAGED AT SOURCE.

  A/6

This A/6 PLOW CRUSH AT SOURCE specimen was found at the top of a seven-foot snowplow pile in its native SOURCE lot. A/6 carts are usually not disposed of by SOURCE agents until the snow pile has melted.

  B/12
   B/14 B/17

This B/5 ON/AS BUSINESS PROPERTY, B/14 ARCHAIC specimen was found in what appears to be a storeroom in a hotel.

 B/12

This B/12 SIMPLE VANDALISM specimen was found along a riverbank. It is likely that the vandal or vandals intended to send the cart into the water but were unsuccessful due to the thick vegetation.

 B/1 B/18

 B/3 SU

 A/4

This A/4 DAMAGED AT SOURCE is slightly unusual in that it has been returned to the line of carts at the SOURCE building. It will most probably transition to B/19 IN/AS REFUSE at the hands of the SOURCE agents.

 L B/3 **R** B/2

 B/12

B/1

This specimen was found approximately one mile from its SOURCE. As with most B/1 OPEN TRUE carts, it is virtually impossible to differentiate from an A/9 REMOTE FALSE.

  B/3 B/14 B/19

 A/6 A/7

 B/15 B/17

This B/3 FRAGMENT was found in a pile of refuse behind a SOURCE building at the edge of a GAP space. The color of the plastic indicated that it was not native to the nearby SOURCE, but rather to a SOURCE that closed in the Buffalo area six years prior to documentation.

 B/15 SU

 B/14 B/18

 B/15

This specimen appears to have been abandoned when the opening in the fence proved too small to pass through. There is a shopping plaza on the other side of the fence; the small openings keep carts from leaving and prevent the entry of B/7 TRANSIENT IMPOSTER carts.

B/19

This group of B/19 IN/AS REFUSE specimens were found in a Dumpster on their native SOURCE lot. Despite still being at their SOURCE, they are TRUE STRAYS due to their irreversible situation.

  B/12

This specimen, viewed from a bridge, was pushed down an embankment in an act of B/12 SIMPLE VANDALISM.

  A/2

   B/5 B/18

 B/5 B/14

This B/5 ON/AS BUSINESS PROPERTY, B/14 ARCHAIC specimen was found being used by the staff in a large, multiuse building. The SOURCE from which it originated closed down 16 years prior to documentation.

 B/12

 B/7 B/22

PLEASE DO NOT LEAVE CHILD UNATTENDED

NO   NO   YES

ALWAYS USE SEAT BELT

A/4

This A/4 DAMAGED AT SOURCE specimen appears to have been laterally crushed in an encounter with a car or truck.

  A/9

It is difficult to know whether or not these A/9 REMOTE FALSE carts were pushed over in an act of B/12 SIMPLE VANDALISM or if they were intentionally tipped over so as to be kept from rolling into the street.

 B/15

 B/4 B/18 SU

 B/2 SU

 B/7 B/10

 B/15

This specimen was found on the grounds of an abandoned housing project. The severity of the damage suggests that it is either a B/10 PLOW CRUSH or B/20 BULLDOZED. Without specific evidence proving one or the other, only the B/2 DAMAGED designation has been assigned.

A/4

A/4 DAMAGED AT SOURCE carts are most easily found by looking behind SOURCE buildings. A/4 carts are usually marginalized to a specific SOURCE area by SOURCE agents.

 B/5 SU

This B/5 ON/AS BUSINESS PROPERTY specimen was found in use at a roadside produce market in central Florida. The tag on the side of the cart reading "Mustards $2.50" indicates that the cart was being used as a display container. If the business were using the cart in a conventional manner (for the use of the customer) it would be classified as B/6 ASSIMILATED.

 B/7

 B/3 B/12 B/14

B/15

A/2 A/6

A/3

These specimens were found in a wooded GAP space between a busy city street and an interstate on-ramp in Hartford, Connecticut. While it is often difficult to determine the difference between B/12 SIMPLE VANDALISM and B/15 GAP MARGINALIZATION, the heavy cart-activity around this GAP space made keeping carts out of the way of traffic a likely motive for acts of B/15.

↖ B/16 B/17

This B/17 REMOTE GROUP appears to be the result of multiple acts of B/16 EDGE MARGINALIZATION originating from an adjacent municipal housing project where numerous B/4 ON/AS PERSONAL PROPERTY carts can be found regularly.

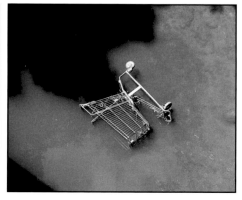

   B/4 SU

These B/4 ON/AS PERSONAL PROPERTY specimens (note the yellow specimen on the top balcony) were documented in an apartment building in Honolulu, Hawaii. This type of B/4 situation has been observed in Eastern North America but not photographically documented.

   A/2 B/9

   B/12 SU

This specimen was found in a marshy area at the edge of a vacant lot that connects to a shopping plaza. It is part of a linear A/8 MIXED GROUP that stretches 70 feet along a two-foot drop-off. The visible specimen appears to have been situated via A/2 PLAZA DRIFT and an act of B/16 EDGE MARGINALIZATION. (Other specimens from this site can be found on pp.116–117.)

The specimen on the left is an A/2 PLAZA DRIFT, B/18 AS REFUSE RECEPTACLE. The specimen on the right is a B/7 TRANSIENT IMPOSTER, B/14 ARCHAIC, B/18 AS REFUSE RECEPTACLE. It is not uncommon to find such complex situations in and around shopping plazas.

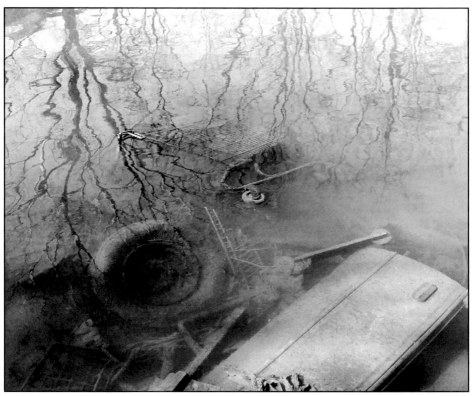

This specimen, a relatively typical example of water-related B/12 SIMPLE VANDALISM, has been observed resting in this location for more than three years. Note that there are multiple B/3 FRAGMENTS in the foreground.

 B/4

This specimen was found in Union Square in Manhattan. B/4 ON/AS PERSONAL PROPERTY in the form of appropriation by the homeless is the most visible TYPE in Manhattan. This often gives New Yorkers the mistaken impression that most stray cart activity is caused by homeless people.

 B/5 SU

 B/2 B/14

↖ B/15 B/21

Found in an urban GAP space, this B/15 GAP MARGINALIZATION specimen will likely transition to B/21 NATURALIZATION, barring a repurposing of the site.

The specimen on the left is a B/14 ARCHAIC cart that has been B/6 ASSIMILATED by a nearby thrift store. The clue that it has been assimilated is the worn off blue paint around the logo. SOURCES that assimilate carts often obscure the original logo.

    B/3 B/8 SU

This specimen is an extreme example of a B/8 STRUCTURALLY MODIFIED cart. The upper structure of a stray cart has been sawed apart to be used as a fence around a private garden that extends onto the sidewalk of a busy street.

  B/4

  A/9

B/2 B/14 B/19 SU

The proximity of the specimen to discarded mattresses and other refuse not visible in this image enables the B/19 designation. The B/14 ARCHAIC TYPE can be assigned to a SOURCE UNKNOWN specimen when the cart model can be determined to be out of use in the region.

   B/12 SU

It is sometimes difficult to determine the transitional potential of carts found in urban waterways. If left alone, they transition to B/21 NATURALIZATION. However, periodic urban cleanup initiatives can lead to the mass removal of carts from the water. Once removed, most carts are then transitioned to B/19 IN/AS REFUSE.

  B/2

  B/15

 A/4

The removal of A/4 DAMAGED AT SOURCE carts from the SOURCE lot to the rear of the building usually happens quickly. This specimen was documented while still in front of its SOURCE building.

 A/8

  B/12 B/21 SU

These specimens were found in a marshy area at the edge of a vacant lot adjacent to a shopping plaza (see p. 103/A). The site, ranging over 70 feet along the edge of a two-foot drop-off, appears to hold as many as 30 carts, although it is difficult to know for certain, given the thickness of the vegetation and marsh conditions.

This A/2 PLAZA DRIFT, A/4 DAMAGED AT SOURCE specimen was probably crushed accidentally by a truck backing into the loading dock. Subsequent snowfall and the formation of ice led to the B/9 SNOW IMMOBILIZATION situation.

 B/4 SU

This B/4 ON/AS PERSONAL PROPERTY specimen was found in the backyard of a private home.

 A/8

 B/15

B/12 B/14 B/21 SU

This specimen is an unusual example of B/12 SIMPLE VANDALISM. The cart was dropped off a bridge to become wedged between the bridge abutment and the rock face. Over the years, possibly decades, multiple levels of debris have accumulated on top of the cart.

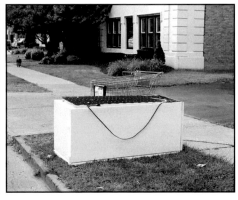

   A/1 B/12

This specimen, found on its native SOURCE lot, appears to have been pushed down the stairs in an act of B/12 SIMPLE VANDALISM.

  A/6

  B/19

This B/8 STRUCTURALLY MODIFIED specimen has been altered for use as a toolbox. The lower structure of the cart has been outfitted with a wider, flatter platform with containers to hold assorted hardware.

B/12

This specimen was found in a creek that runs behind multiple SOURCES. The creek area has consistently high levels of B/12 SIMPLE VANDALISM activity.

It is difficult to determine the course of events that led these specimens to be found near this expressway off-ramp. Found close to their native SOURCE, the carts may have been pushed down the off-ramp in an act of B/12 SIMPLE VANDALISM and then marginalized in an orderly fashion by a well-meaning citizen. The snow appears to have fallen after the main sequence of events.

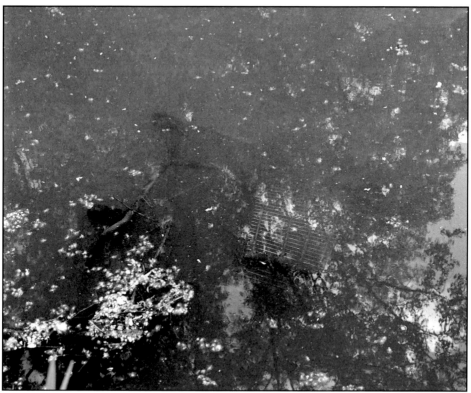

   B/12 SU

Unfortunately for the casual cart observer, the majority of water-oriented B/12 SIMPLE VANDALISM or B/13 COMPLEX VANDALISM specimens are obscured by dark or deep water.

   B/2 B/15

  A/8

Once they rust, metal B/11 TRAIN DAMAGED carts become difficult to distinguish from the natural environment. It takes a keen eye to separate the lines of this specimen from the thorny vines that entangle it.

  B/3 B/12 B/14

This is a rare occurrence of a B/3 FRAGMENT lodged in the branches of a tall bush. The specimen is suspended approximately five feet above the ground; it was most likely placed there via an act of B/12 SIMPLE VANDALISM. At the time of this writing, an intact cart has never been found lodged in a tree.

 A/6

 B/2 B/18

These specimens were found 20 feet from a bus stop. The snow on the ground made pushing the carts all the way to the stop too difficult.

Both of these specimens are B/18 AS/REFUSE RECEPTACLE, B/19 IN/AS REFUSE. The specimen on the left is also a B/22 WHEEL LOCK STRAY. Despite the wheel-locking mechanism, this specimen was found at least a mile from any SOURCE that uses this model of cart.

 B/8 B/15

These specimens were found in a vacant lot. The fact that both carts are missing their two front wheels strongly suggests that the wheels were purposefully removed for practical use in an act of B/8 STRUCTURAL MODIFICATION.

 B/15 B/18

 B/16

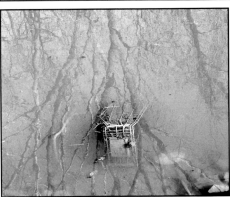

   B/5 SU

These B/5 ON/AS BUSINESS PROPERTY carts were found being used as merchandise displays in a North Florida souvenir shop.

   B/12 SU

   A/2 B/9

B/3 B/14 B/20

This specimen was found on an old railroad bed. The track had been torn up some years before, leaving a wide empty swath of elevated land. While it is possible that this B/3 FRAGMENT was initially damaged by a train, it appears to have been placed in its current situation by the bulldozing process that cleared the railroad ties. Similar B/20 BULLDOZED specimens were found in the area.

   B/2 B/15

This B/2 DAMAGED, B/15 GAP MARGINALIZED specimen was found in a GAP space.

   B/4 SU

   B/7 B/18

  B/7

The cart in the foreground is the B/7 TRANSIENT IMPOSTER.

   B/15 SU

   B/2 B/19

This B/5 ON/AS BUSINESS PROPERTY, B/8 STRUCTURALLY MODIFIED specimen was found next to a factory that was in the process of being torn down. The banner tape tied to it warns that there is asbestos on the site. It was probably modified for a specific function in the factory.

This B/3 FRAGMENT, B/12 SIMPLE VANDALISM, B/14 ARCHAIC specimen was found in a creek that runs through an urban area. At the time of documentation, the SOURCE of origin had been closed for five years.

  A/6

Although the snowplow damage to these specimens is slight (note the separation of the plastic basket from the top of the metal frame), they still fall under the definition A/6 PLOW CRUSH AT SOURCE.

 A/9 B/18

 B/2 B/9 B/15 B/18

B/5

In Manhattan, B/4 ON/AS PERSONAL PROPERTY and B/5 ON/AS BUSINESS PROPERTY carts are closely guarded. It is common to find carts locked up or kept behind fences.

B/5 B/14

B/1 B/2

A/8 B/9

This B/5 ON/AS BUSINESS PROPERTY, B/14 ARCHAIC was found being used by workers who were repairing walls in a large building.

This B/3 FRAGMENT, B/11 TRAIN DAMAGED was found near a set of railroad tracks that run behind a shopping plaza.

B/5 B/17 B/18 B/19

This specimen was found with a number of other carts in a scrap yard. It is part of a B/17 REMOTE GROUP and it is functioning as a refuse receptacle in an intentional and practical way. This allows the B/5 ON/AS BUSINESS PROPERTY and B/18 AS REFUSE RECEPTACLE TYPE designations. It is also in the scrap yard as scrap, allowing the B/19 IN/AS REFUSE designation.

 A/4

This specimen was found behind its native SOURCE building.

 B/1

A/8

 B/7 B/15

This appears to be a mild case of B/15 GAP MARGINALIZATION. The B/7 TRANSIENT IMPOSTER has been marginalized just enough to keep it from being a nuisance.

 B/1 B/2

 A/1 B/12

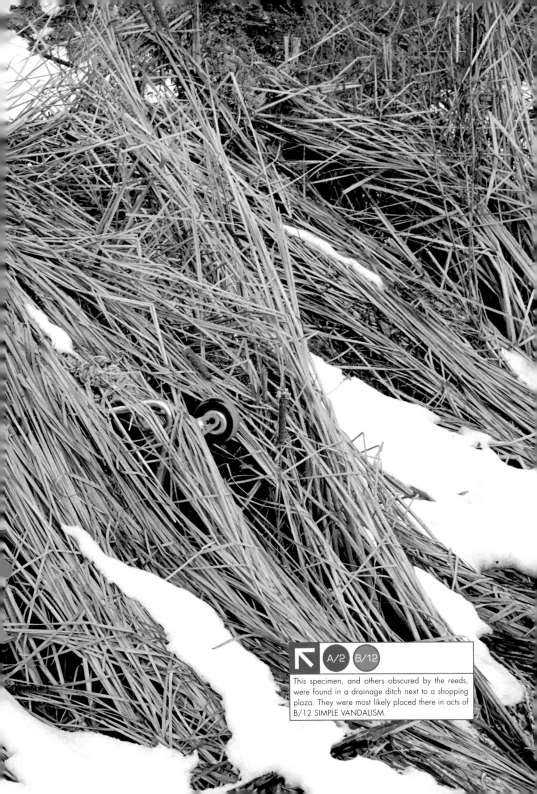

This specimen, and others obscured by the reeds, were found in a drainage ditch next to a shopping plaza. They were most likely placed there in acts of B/12 SIMPLE VANDALISM.

This B/15 GAP MARGINALIZATION, B/19 IN/AS REFUSE specimen was found in the GAP space between a set of railroad tracks and the backyards of a long row of residential homes.

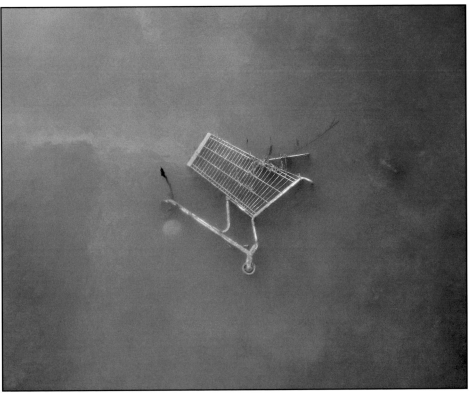

   B/12 B/21

This specimen represents the common combination of B/12 SIM-PLE VANDALISM and B/21 NATURALIZATION. A return visit to the site, after the initial documentation, found that the currents of the creek had moved the cart 50 feet downstream.

  B/1

  B/9

B/12

The mud and plant life on this specimen suggest that it has spent some time submerged in the water. It may have been pulled out of the creek as part of a cleanup effort.

  B/2 B/15 B/19 SU

This specimen B/19 IN/AS REFUSE was found in an illegal dump site in an urban GAP space.

 B/1 B/15

 A/4

This specimen is an example a B/8 STRUCTURALLY MODIFIED cart. When the lower structure is taken from a stray cart it is often used to build a new cart, customized to perform a specific function.

 A/11

This A/11 FALSE GROUP, found in a suburb of Cleveland, Ohio, appears to have been gathered by citizens with the expectation that the SOURCE agents will recover the carts.

Found near a set of train tracks, this B/3 FRAGMENT was almost certainly the result of a B/11 TRAIN DAMAGED situation.

 A/2

This A/2 PLAZA DRIFT has been used as a table of sorts for employees on break. Note the chips and salsa on the seat.

A/3 B/9

B/14 B/17 B/18

B/7

This B/7 TRANSIENT IMPOSTER was found at the edge of a SOURCE lot in West Hartford, Connecticut. Its precarious position at the top of an eight-foot wall greatly increases its susceptibility to acts of B/12 SIMPLE VANDLISM.

NIAGARA FALLS

ANALYZING A COMPLEX VANDALISM SUPER SITE

Sites featuring repeated shopping cart vandalism are fairly common in Eastern North America, but few are as dramatic and multilayered as the one found less than a mile downriver from the Niagara cataracts in Niagara Falls, New York.

The site is in Niagara Reservation State Park, a thin strip of land between the Robert Moses Parkway and the Niagara River. The park features hiking trails that descend 200 feet down the steep incline of the gorge to the river. The park is approximately one hundred yards across the parkway from a residential neighborhood that contains several SOURCES. A footbridge and an access road (see p. 168/B) connect the neighborhood to the trail system. The focal point of cart vandalism is a rocky ledge that overlooks the gorge (see p. 168/A). Carts are pushed off of the ledge to fall 50 feet to a steep incline (see diagram). The site appears to have been a hot spot for vandalism activity for several decades. In addition to shopping carts, the cascading field of detritus below the cliff (see p. 169/A/B/C and pp. 170–171) also includes cars, tires, rugs, mattresses, street signs, bicycles, appliances, wood, rocks, pipes, and chunks of concrete. The repeated use of the site, the naturally occurring rock slides, and the breaking off of boulders from the rock face create the conditions that lead to B/21 NATURALIZATION. Many carts have been crushed or buried by boulders, rocks, and other debris.

Although the residential neighborhood is close to the site, all specimens found here are B/13 COMPLEX VANDALISM due to the deliberate actions one must take to situate a cart at the edge of the gorge. In the shortest scenario, a vandal takes four steps to arrive at the edge with a cart. The drop-off point is not en route to anywhere one would travel with a shopping cart for any practical purpose; this reinforces the hypothesis that this site represents chronic B/13, and not B/15 GAP MARGINALIZATION or B/19 IN/AS REFUSE.

Due to the previously described conditions, almost all of the specimens found here share at least the same four TYPE designations: B/2 DAMAGED, B/13 COMPLEX VANDALISM, B/17 REMOTE GROUP, and B/21 NATURALIZATION. The two variable additions to this are B/3 FRAGMENT and B/14 ARCHAIC.

RIVER GORGE →

↘ NIAGARA RIVER GORGE SITE DIAGRAM

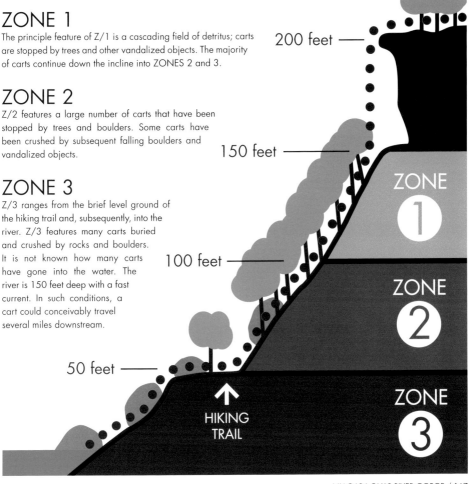

ZONE 1

The principle feature of Z/1 is a cascading field of detritus; carts are stopped by trees and other vandalized objects. The majority of carts continue down the incline into ZONES 2 and 3.

ZONE 2

Z/2 features a large number of carts that have been stopped by trees and boulders. Some carts have been crushed by subsequent falling boulders and vandalized objects.

ZONE 3

Z/3 ranges from the brief level ground of the hiking trail and, subsequently, into the river. Z/3 features many carts buried and crushed by rocks and boulders. It is not known how many carts have gone into the water. The river is 150 feet deep with a fast current. In such conditions, a cart could conceivably travel several miles downstream.

200 feet ——

150 feet ——

100 feet ——

50 feet ——

HIKING TRAIL ↑

ZONE ①

ZONE ②

ZONE ③

Although carts have been found in other locations in the Niagara Gorge, the cliff ledge, pictured above, is by far the most frequently used drop-off point. This is due, in part, to the fact that the rocky overhang provides the vandal with a good view of the vandalized cart's fall and subsequent destruction.

The underpass is part of an access road that connects the nearby neighborhood to the hiking trails. It is the most likely entry point for vandals with carts.

A gravel path leads to a short dirt trail to the drop-off point.

ZONE 1

These images are views of the cascading debris field from the middle of ZONE 1.

ZONE
2

↖ B/2 B/13 B/17 B/21

This photograph of the upper part of Z/2 illustrates the high density of vandalized objects at the gorge site. It is unknown how many carts occupy the site. To find out would require a massive excavation of all three Zones.

ZONE ③

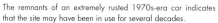

The remnants of an extremely rusted 1970s-era car indicates
that the site may have been in use for several decades.

ZONE
3

 B/2 B/13 B/17 B/21 SU

The Z/3 specimens have been buried in a rock slide.

The cart handle in the lower right image may be the top of a buried cart or merely a B/3 FRAGMENT.

 B/3 B/13 B/17 B/21 SU

 B/3 B/13 B/17 B/21 SU

This specimen was crushed by a large piece of pipe. It is unlikely that it will ever be moved from its current resting place.

⭘ APPENDIX A: RELATED PHENOMENA

There are three related phenoma that, at times, follow some of the same transitional patterns as stray shopping carts and occupy the same spaces.

STRAY PLASTIC BAGS ⭘

Stray plastic bags share with stray shopping carts mobility and a common SOURCE. They differ, however, in that, unlike shopping carts, they are unlikely to be reused. They are commonly found in the branches of trees, in bushes, and on fences. The ability to be swept away by the wind gives them an even greater range of travel than stray shopping carts.

DISCARDED CAR TIRES ⭘

Because tires cannot be thrown out in the trash, they are often dumped in the same GAP spaces to which shopping carts are marginalized. They also appear to be susceptible to acts of SIMPLE VANDALISM, particularly those involving inclines and bodies of water. Tires are often a sign that stray shopping carts may be in the vicinity. Images of stray carts and tires together can be found throughout this guide.

STRAY TRAFFIC CONES ⭘

Traffic cones are susceptible to acts of SIMPLE and COMPLEX VANDALISM in much the same way shopping carts are. They are frequently thrown into bodies of water. Of the related phenomena, the cones are the only ones that are subject to a FALSE STRAY / TRUE STRAY transitional pattern.